WORKING FOR YOURSELF AS A GRAPHIC DESIGNER

How to start, set up and run your own successful business as a graphic designer

KATHRYN ANNICE ROBERTS

Orders: Please contact Kathryn Roberts

You can also order via the e mail address
kathrynrobertsdesign@outlook.com

ISBN: 978-1-5272-6178-5

First published 2020

Copyright © 2020 Kathryn Annice Roberts.

Contents

INTRODUCTION

From one graphic designer to another, I welcome you to this book. In this guide, I'll teach you how to start up on your own as a designer, and give you an indication of the work and determination that you'll need to put in. I believe that the reason you have picked up this book is because you are potentially in the same position I was in a few years ago, where I had my heart set on starting up and running a business in graphic design, and was looking for help in doing so.

This book will give you first-hand insight into my journey from a shy, small town girl to starting up and running my own successful business as a graphic designer. Every method that I write about is a method that I have tried either successfully or unsuccessfully. I will explain how these methods have got me to where I am today and how you can apply them to your own business to make a success of it. My goal is to give you first-hand knowledge into what you should do, and what you should avoid, whilst setting up your graphic design business. I will also give you an insight into things that you may not have considered, at this early stage in your career.

My journey into the world of design began at a very young age, from my love of the art, media and technology subjects in school, leading to the completion of my GCSE's and A Levels in Art and Media, to my childhood dream of graduating from University with a degree I am passionate about and extremely proud of, which is Graphic Communication. The past decade has been such a whirlwind of hard work and motivation, and I can proudly say it has resulted in something I never thought would happen to me at such a young age, starting my own successful business as a graphic designer.

Coming from a family of strong, talented businesspeople, I have always carried the enthusiasm and motivation to make whatever challenge I face a success – being incredibly stubborn also helps (sometimes)! I don't like to see myself as 'following a path' as such, as to me, following a path suggests a lack of control of your own intentions. To me, if you're choosing to start up your own business, you are MAKING your path, not following it. As you are a designer, see it as the chance to DESIGN your own path and success without any limitations or guidelines – arguably every graphic designer's dream! Looking at it like this should mean you never tire of creating this path, as it is YOUR life and YOUR passion and with my help, you will make your passion into a happy, exciting and successful career and lifestyle. In my opinion, you have chosen the best field in the world, a field that is constantly evolving and you have chosen to become a part of this exciting evolution, so embrace it, face the challenges and enjoy every moment!

I have divided this book into five sections, so that it covers all the information, skills and confidence that I strongly believe are needed to successfully start up and run your business in a convenient and easy to read way. Section one is a first-hand guide to 'providing a quality service'. This section should help you to decide on what services you will offer your own clients, and how you plan to successfully reach your target audience based on my own experiences in business. This section will also explain the benefits of building good relationships with clients, learning the extremely important art of good communication, learning how to deal with complaints and how to stop yourself from saying that one word that could potentially cost you a sale – to find out what this one word is, keep on reading!

Section two will cover my views on how health, fitness and mindset can affect the success of yourself and your business. I will give you my top tips on how you can stay fit, healthy and happy whilst working at a computer 9am – 5pm, as well as how to avoid having to sit at your computer 9 – 5! I will teach you how to manage distractions and how to manage stress and mindfulness, much like how yourself and others can highly benefit from outsourcing work to take away stress and pressure where it is not necessary. Everything you need to know about outsourcing will be covered in section three.

Finally, section four will cover the gold mine that is social media, giving tips and examples across some of the many popular social media platforms, and section five will cover the marketing and business side. This includes the practical stuff which will be the main structure of your business. It will include what you need to know about establishing your target audience, VAT registration, marketing and advertising. These two sections combined will be a guide of how to keep your graphic design business in profit.

Every morning I wake up looking forward to learning and discovering new tips and tricks about the industry, and I strongly believe that if you use the advice and tips that I've given you in this book, your successful graphic design business is just around the corner. Success is a choice we make. If you are passionate enough and willing it put in the work, there is every reason to believe that your business will succeed.

Kathryn Roberts

SECTION 1
PROVIDING A
QUALITY SERVICE

Whether or not you consider yourself to be a 'people person', developing good relationships with your clients is a fundamental requirement for any successful businessperson. You must be able to communicate clearly and efficiently, manage the expectations of both yourself and your clients and ALWAYS deliver on your promises. This section will fully explain each of these statements, using hidden tips and examples to ensure you are providing the best possible service for your clients and building that success for your business.

When I say you need to have a good relationship with your client, I don't necessarily mean you need to be best friends with them. In fact, I almost discourage you from becoming best friends with your clients, as this could possibly lead to false assumptions that you will do favours and give out freebies or 'mate's rates', and this is certainly not what you started your business for. So, having a relationship that is too close can sometimes be just as toxic as not having a good relationship with them at all.

You don't even need to have met your clients in person – some of my biggest, longest standing clients, I have never even spoken to face to face and don't entirely know what they look like, but over time have gotten to know them on a professional and under-standing level that works for the both of us. You need to find a middle ground and build that mutual respect and appreciation without pushing any limits. As long as there is good communi-cation at all times, and you understand each other, there is no reason why your relationship can't be purely over email or over the phone.

You may find some of your clients to be awkward and unpleasant to work with, but you cannot ever let that show; you must always communicate with professionalism, understanding, empathy and a friendly tone. This means you also need to develop a thick skin, if you don't already have one. What I mean by this is that at least one point in your career, you will most definitely find yourself dealing with clients that come across as rude and ignorant of the hard work you are putting into their project, and you need to learn to not let criticism and negative comments affect your professionalism. You have to remain calm and collected at all times and put the client's happiness above any negative feelings you may have towards the situation at that time. I have found that one of the best ways to avoid these situations is to let your client assume your limits, not know them.

What do I mean by this? Well I actually mean it literally word for word. When talking to a client for the first time, your goal is to, between you, pinpoint exactly what service the client is expecting, what the outcome will be, the purpose of the outcome and when that outcome will be ready. During the process of this, you need to let the client know that you will complete the required job for an agreed price in an agreed timeframe. What you want your client to assume is that you will go above and beyond to deliver what they want...and more, so you need to demonstrate this in order to really impress them.

A lot of the time clients don't really know exactly what they want from you, which is why they hired a graphic designer in the first place. They expect you to know what is best for them and they will always want it delivered as quickly as possible and to the highest standard, which as a graphic designer, should not come as a surprise to you. You are currently starting out and in the process of establishing your business, so now is the prime opportunity to show your clients exactly what you can do, set your standards and start building your positive reputation. Getting this right at the beginning of your career is crucial, as it's often difficult to bounce back from a bad first impression.

Let's give an example scenario, you are theoretically meeting with a client who is starting up their own hair salon. They tell you they have no idea what to call the hair salon, what they want their logo and brand to look like, but they know that they want to attract young women and like the colours pink and gold, and so want them incorporated in the brand somehow. They ask you what you recommend they need from you in order to advertise their business and make it a success. Now, as a graphic designer, you should know how to answer this, but don't put too much pressure on the situation. You don't want to overload them with information they don't understand, but you also don't want them to think you don't know what you're talking about. Instead, you need to find that middle ground, and here's what I do:

Whether it's face to face, over the phone or over email, I ALWAYS start by asking the client for as much information about their business as possible, so I can take notes to help me when it comes to doing the work later on. This information could include target audience, location, theme, business size and scope for advertising. Following on from this, I cannot emphasise enough the importance of having all this information in an accessible written form for both yourself, and your client, to refer to at any point. This also means that if, for any reason, there is a disagreement or misunderstanding between yourself and the client, you have a written form of evidence to refer back to. This applies to any form of communication throughout the process, as quick and convenient as phone calls can be, I believe that email communication is always a good idea when discussing terms and ground for your work. However, you will sometimes need to communicate face to face or over the phone and so, ALWAYS have a pen and paper handy to take notes, and when the conversation is finished, agree to send each other a text or email which covers the key points made in the conversation. This is so important.

Another good tip I will suggest is having a list of questions ready to ask them, or even a questionnaire for them to fill out. This is a quick and simple way for you to get to know what your client is looking for, it also gives them a basis to understand what it is you need to know from them, as a lot of the time, people won't know what you expect from them, it's up to you to know that. Here's an example of one of my client questionnaires that can be adapted to suit any client or project:

KARD
Kathryn Annice Roberts
Design

Client Design Questionnaire

Client Name

Address

Tel.

Email

Company Name
(if applicable)

Wording of Logo required

Preferred Colour(s)

Target age(s) of audience

☐   ☐   ☐   ☐
N/A   Under 12   13-17   Adult

Do you have a Brand Identity? (Y/N) ☐

If yes, please send details with this form

Intended uses of Logo

Letter Head	Website	Small Items eg pens/mugs	Large Items eg Vehicles	Other (please specify)
☐	☐	☐	☐	

Please supply any additional information you feel is relevant to the design

Please complete as many sections of this questionnaire a possible and return to
kathrynrobertsdesign@outlook.com together with any additional information.

You will receive the first draft within [5] working days of receiving the completed questionnaire and other relevant information.

The price for one Logo is   £

The price for additional Logo is   £

Now that you have this client scenario in your head, I will go back to my previous statement 'let your client assume your limits, not know them', and explain how to easily apply this to every situation with a client.

As you are going through and working out what the client is looking for, and making notes on what to research later on, the customer asks you the dreaded but inevitable question: 'How long do you think this will take to design?'

Timelines

When giving timelines, you need to be realistic for yourself and your own capabilities, but you also need to make the client feel like they are getting the best deal from you. People will naturally want a high-quality outcome in a short space of time for a low price, but this isn't always possible, and you shouldn't ever put too much pressure on yourself to deliver this. What works wonders for me, is deciding realistically how long the piece of work expected from the client will take, figuring out a price based on that, and overdelivering.

For example, this client may want a new logo for their new hair salon which you personally decide will take you two days to do. You tell the client you will get them a couple of design ideas done and sent over within a week, but in that week, you get three logo ideas designed, as well as a few examples of what each design would look like on various marketing materials. As the client will be expecting the designs within a week, doing this extra bit of work is going above and beyond to give the client exactly what they asked for...PLUS MORE!

At this point, you may be wondering 'What's the point of giving the client more than they are paying for? Why should I waste time on producing work that the client may not even want or appreciate?' The way you should be looking at this, is that the client may look at these extra designs and decide that they want you to also design and print business cards, leaflets, merchandise and even a website for them, purely because you decided to put those extra few hours into convincing them that you are what their business needs. You should go into every project with this attitude, because you have the capability to produce the highest quality work for a reasonable price, and it may just be that the client didn't ask you to produce this extra work because it just didn't cross their mind that they wanted/needed it. It is your job to convince them that you are the one that can help make their brand thrive and they need to believe that they do need these extra materials. Also, everyone likes to feel like they're getting good value for money! Give it a try, and if it turns out you don't make more money from it, you have just created more content for your portfolio which other future clients may take an interest in. Nothing you produce will ever go to waste! If you are for any reason unable to produce more than what was agreed with the client, just be sure to give them and yourself a realistic timeline, keep them in the loop and always deliver your promises, no matter what!

One effective way of ensuring that you are putting the right number of hours into a project is by having a timesheet on hand to fill out as you complete certain tasks throughout the day/week. This is something I learnt from my first agency job and I've kept it going with my own business. There are thousands of apps and websites for tracking your time out there, but the one I am most familiar with is Harvest (www.getharvest.com).

Harvest is extremely easy to use and although it is not free, you get a 30-day free trial to allow you to familiarise yourself with it and decide whether it is worth continuing with. The way Harvest works is you add jobs that you are working on and are able to set a physical timer to run in the background until you have finished working on that project, this allows you to get exact timescales documented and to stop yourself from committing more time to one project when there is another project on standby that should possibly be getting more time. Harvest works wonders especially in an agency setting where there are multiple people involved. But even though you are working for yourself, it could be useful to have someone to hold you accountable for your timekeeping, who can also view your timesheet if they have a Harvest account too. Just don't forget to stop the timer when you have finished working on something, you need to keep your timesheets as accurate as possible at all times to avoid confusion!

If you don't wish to pay for a timekeeping platform, that is fair enough. Another extremely simple way of doing this for free is a simple pen and paper. Dedicate a nice new notebook or week-to-view diary to timekeeping and make a list of the projects you have going on week by week. If you're using a week-to-view diary then the days will already be laid out for you, but if you're using a notebook, all you have to do it separate the pages into each day of the week and simply write down the time spent on each project next to the relevant one.

Whichever way you decide works best for you, I highly recommend sticking to it and incorporating it into your daily work routine, as you don't want to fall behind on your deadlines. Stay focused and stay organised at all times and there will be no room for anything to go wrong.

Communication

Working in any business involves a strong amount of communication with others in some form, whether it's communicating directly with clients, colleagues or suppliers. But when you are self-employed, YOU are the face of the brand. YOU carry all the responsibility for the reputation of your business, and so it is important to present yourself in a way that all potential clients, outsourcers etc. will respect you and want to continue to work with you.

The final and most important tip from this section is to communicate yourself politely and timely. Every email requires a response, even if you don't believe it does. For example, a client may email you simply to thank you for doing a great job, the courteous thing to do would be to respond with a simple 'you're welcome, I look forward to hopefully working together again in the future.' It's simple and potentially seems pointless, however the client will see that as respectful, friendly and someone keen to please – which I'm sure you are!

'Timely' is another word I want you to always consider during the process of communication. Even if you are busy, a simple acknowledgment email or text message along the lines of 'Hi Liz, thank you for your message, I just want to let you know that I am tied up right now, but I will respond thoroughly as soon as possible.' This kind of polite communication goes a long way and makes you look incredibly professional.

Reviews

I'd now like to get onto the next crucial topic within this section... reviews! I will cover various review platforms for you to be aware of later on in the book. No one likes to hear negative feedback or criticism in any form, it can knock your confidence, make you sad, angry, stressed or all of the above! It is arguably worse having negative feedback written in the form of a review for the public to see, and one bad review could cost you a sale or even a client. So, you need to be extremely careful about how to manage your services in order to avoid those negative reviews on your website, social media blogs etc...and here's how.

To begin with, everything I have written in this section so far and realistically, everything in this book is a guide to a successful business as a graphic designer and so if you read carefully and follow my advice, there should not be any reason why anyone would leave you a negative review. However, it is known that people leave negative reviews to businesses they may not have even had contact with or worked with. While this might be completely unfair, sometimes you have no control over this. For example, my business page on Facebook was left a 1* rating by someone I have never even heard of or had any kind of contact with before. That 1* rating has unnecessarily brought down my overall star rating and there's annoyingly nothing I can do to challenge it. Whether something like this happens to you or not, there are unfortunately, a lot of the time, no ways of removing these reviews and ratings from the public eye, and so you have to focus on building up those positive reviews to show your potential clients that your business is outstanding and worth the sale.

If you are in a position where you receive a negative review, whether you agree with it or not, it is crucial that you respond to it in a polite and professional manner. Your response should show that you have sympathetically acknowledged the review and you should highlight how you intend to resolve the issue. Do not appear defensive and always revert back to the typical saying 'the customer is always right'. Another thing you must avoid at all costs is a fob off. Doing this will not only get you respect from the unhappy client but will show everyone else that views it that you are trustworthy, genuine and looking out for your clients' best interests. Remember, everything you share online is in the public eye, so you need to remain professional and sympathetic at all times. If you don't, this will most likely cost you.

We will all at some point encounter a bad experience with a service, whether it's a holiday, a restaurant or a designer like yourself. Nine times out of ten, if you put a negative review on a company platform, they will respond almost immediately with the standard 'Hi Katie, thank you for your review. We are sorry you have had this experience, feel free to send us a message...' and in my opinion, this is not how you should respond to an unhappy customer, as in my experience, it can be seen as a way of brushing the problem under the carpet, and it almost always ends in the customer becoming more frustrated.

How I recommend that you respond to a review is something similar to as follows: 'Hi Katie, thank you so much for your feedback. I'm deeply apologetic that my services did not reach your expectations and am eager to put this right in any way that I can, I will give you a call today to discuss how we can put this right to avoid disappointment in the future, what time is best for you to chat?'

Let's go through my response phrase by phrase. I begin with thanking them for the feedback. Like the previous example, this is a good and simple way to let the customer know you have read and acknowledged the review. Now, instead of the old automated-sounding 'sorry you had this experience', try and add a bit more sympathy, acknowledge that you are in the wrong and highlight your willingness to put the situation right as soon as possible. Instead of leaving it to them to message you (because I am pretty certain that leaving it to them will just aggravate them more and push them to want to continue making the issue public), tell them you will call them that day, and make sure you prioritise this! In these situations, especially, a phone call is so much more appreciated and valued than a text or email, as it shows the customer that you are willing to put your hands up and resolve the issue without hiding behind a keyboard. Talking on the phone also gives both yourself and the client the opportunity to physically talk about and resolve the problem without any misunderstandings or misinterpretations that can easily happen over text or email. I also finish the response by asking the customer what time suits them, this reassures them that you are serious about wanting the issue resolved and are not willing to make the old 'I tried to call but there was no answer' excuse.

There are ways of managing your services to ensure that you receive so many positive reviews that the one negative one is potentially ignored, and your success rate isn't affected. These ways are as mentioned earlier:

- **Building good and mutually respectful relationships with your clients;**
- **Communicating well;**
- **Behaving in a professional and sympathetic manner;**
- **ALWAYS delivering on your promises.**

Following on from this, you need to ensure that your clients know and believe that you are all these things before they even contact you, and this goes down to not only the quality of the finished article, but also the way you advertise yourself and promote your services in order to get the commission in the first place!

If you are still in the process of establishing yourself and your client basis, one thing I strongly advise is not to be shy about asking for feedback and asking your clients to leave you reviews. There is no shame in asking and if you truly believe that you have provided the quality service that you promise your clients, then there is no reason why you do not deserve positive and constructive feedback. When I was first starting out and even to this day, I largely relied on commissions from family and friends, which is a great place to start as these are the people that know you best and know your abilities – all the more better for receiving those good reviews!

As I mentioned in the previous paragraph, start with your friends and family members. By getting their approval of your services, you are ten times more likely to have them singing your praises to their own contacts, who then spread the word to their friends who are conveniently looking for a loyal, true to form designer to create a logo for their new business...and so on, you get the picture! Although written reviews are incredibly important in ensuring that your business gets the success and recognition it deserves, word of mouth can be just as powerful.

To summarise this subsection, I personally believe that pushing for those reviews early on is what will make your business stand out in the future – I don't know about you, but one of the first things I do when looking for a service is head to the reviews section to see what has been said about the business.

Having reviews also makes your business profile look more legit and genuine than having no reviews, as it shows that you are experienced and provide a quality service. Put in the work now and you will be heavily rewarded for it in the future!

Save Your Skin

The next topic I want to cover is arguably more technical and less widely understood by start-ups but is extremely important. This topic is intellectual property – or copyright, and the extreme impor-tance of watermarks and Non-Disclosure Agreements (NDAs), or as I like to call it...saving your skin!

I will cover this topic in more detail in section five and will explain why trademarking your business is so important. I will go through the differences between copyright and trademark and I will explain why trademarking your business is so important. However, in this section I aim to focus solely on the facts about copyright and why you should ALWAYS watermark your work right up to the second that you receive full payment from the client to avoid complications later on.

According to the Intellectual Property Office (IPO), 'copyright gives the creators of certain kinds of materials rights to control ways their material can be used. These rights start as soon as the material is recorded in writing or in any other way.' In other words, everyone has copyright over any piece of original work that they produce, whether it's artistic, musical, dramatic, literary, recorded sound, whether the piece of work is personal, or client commissioned...the list goes on. There is no official registration, everyone is automatically entitled to copyright of their own work.

Now, following on from that, if you create a piece of commissioned work for a client, it is critical that you write up a contract and Non-Disclosure Agreement (NDA) that clearly states that the copyright of the work you have created will only be transferred to the client following full payment of the service.

An NDA, also known as a Confidentiality Agreement (CA) is a legal document that outlines any confidential or mutually agreed terms between people. You do not want to make the same mistake I did early on in my career by failing to present a contract to the client and failing to watermark my designs before sending them, resulting in the client taking my designs without payment and using them. Remember, just because you believe you have formed a good relationship with a client, you must never let your guard down and put yourself at risk of being taken advantage of.

It is ALWAYS worth spending those extra few minutes writing up a contract and adding your name or logo as a watermark on a piece of work.

You may think that as the designer of the work, I am entitled to the intellectual property (copyright) of that work, and to an extent you are correct. However, as I didn't have anything in a written form between myself and the client that had been mutually agreed and signed, the fault technically was with me, and after understanding this, there really is no point in trying to justify it but learning from it is key. After reading this, I now hope that you will be learning from my mistakes and not your own. Look at my own experiences that I am sharing with you and take my advice to ensure you do not go through the same things. Below is an example of a (now discarded) logo option for a client where I have used my KARD Graphic Design watermark.

If you are unsure of how to create a watermark, it is super quick and easy. There are multiple ways of doing it but the way I do it is simply having a 'JPEG' image of my logo repeated, dropping it over the top of the design in photoshop, lowering the opacity of the logo to around 2%, and flattening the image (as seen in the above image). It literally takes 2 minutes and really can save your skin!

In conclusion:

- **ALWAYS make the client read and sign a contract before you begin working with them;**
- **ALWAYS send over any pre-payment designs with a clear watermark using either your company name or logo;**
- **NEVER let your guard down and assume that people will not take advantage of you when they see the opportunity.**

When both yourself and the client are happy that the design is right and full payment has been made, then they should receive the final, high quality version of the design. Remember, by sending the final, unwatermarked design to the client, you are then agreeing to transfer the copyright of that design to them and will no longer own it – if this is what you have chosen to state in your contract. So only send it when everyone is completely happy with this.

If you are in the process of writing up a contract for a client and are struggling with knowing what to include, I recommend creating a standard template that you can slightly alter to each client to save you from having to write a new one for each project, as no matter how different the projects are from each other, the legal requirements will remain the same. This also makes life a lot easier for yourself and saves so much time and energy.

There are lots of contract templates online that are free to use and below is a copy of my standard client agreement that you are also welcome to adapt and use for yourself. Please bear in mind that you are always able to retain the intellectual property upon agreement of both parties, this is purely down to preference and I would suggest getting professional advice if you are unsure of what to do here.

Your contract and NDA should highlight all the points you wish to make to cover your own back and these points should be presented in a clear format to avoid and misinterpretations.

Client Name:
Project Type:
Designer Name:
Designer Email:

KARD

Kathryn Annice Roberts
Design

• As the designer, I agree to produce project materials at the request of the client for fees agreed upon in advance and delivery of the work by an agreed-upon deadline. I agree that I will be the sole author of the work, which will be free of plagiarism, and once the work has been handed to the client, it can be used but not altered in any way. I will be in constant contact with the client during the designing and editing process to ensure the client is completely happy with what I produce.

• Client agrees to pay 50% of the total project cost before any services are provided, and the remaining 50% is to be paid before the final files are delivered. If the parameters of the work change, or if it involves more time than estimated, I will inform the client straight away.

• Upon acceptance of the work, the client accepts responsibility for any further processes in which this work is used (e.g. film outpost, printing, etc.). The designer is not responsible for errors occurring in this work or projects related to this work after acceptance of the work by the client.

• Both parties understand that either the client or designer may terminate the service at any time if, for any reason, the relationship is deemed unsatisfactory. Upon written or verbal cancellation, the client is responsible for payment for all expenses incurred and any work done towards the completion of the project based on the percentage of the project completed that is determined by the designer. Should the client cancel the project following its completion, the client is then responsible for full payment as per the agreed upon estimate plus all expenses incurred. In the event of cancellation, the designer still retains full ownership of all copyrights and original work created.

By signing below, you, as the client agree that you have read, understood and accept these terms.

Client signature: ....

Date: ....

Getting started with a new business and beginning to establish that connection with clients is super exciting but also super challenging, and you want these first encounters to make a good, lasting impression on you and your business. So, take my advice and prepare yourself for all the challenges that will come your way. Remember, failing to prepare is preparing to fail!

Internships

During my time at university, whilst building up KARD Graphic Design and keeping on top of my university projects, I was always on the lookout for work, and this doesn't necessarily mean freelance work for my business. Just because you are building yourself up as a self-employed freelancer, there is no reason why you cannot and should not apply for and take part in internships.

Over the last 3 years I have completed 3 design-related internships of various lengths, all in completely different geographical locations and different areas of design, and I believe that each one of them has helped me massively with the way run my own business as well as the way I approach design. Not to mention the countless skills learnt as well as that extra bit of income. I think that, especially within the first few years of running your business, you should be open minded to internships, as they will not do you any harm, and especially if you are like me, business and income may be running at a relatively slow pace at the beginning, and so all the more reason to find work elsewhere. This not only increases your experience and your portfolio; it teaches you valuable life skills and people skills that you may not learn whilst working for yourself.

One final piece of advice I would like to give to conclude this section is to make the most of EVERY opportunity that comes your way. Be it freelance work, employed work or internships. Don't ever think that you have to turn down an opportunity to work in an agency for a period of time purely because you are running your own business. From my experience of working in agencies, there are so many things that I have learnt that being freelance won't necessarily ever teach me, and I have made so many contacts and had the opportunity to live in some amazing locations through these experiences, it is so worth it! Just remember that when it comes to the paperwork, you must declare all earnings on your tax return – find out more about tax and accounting in section five.

SECTION 2
YOUR HEALTH AND WELLBEING

Having suffered from severe confidence and anxiety issues practically my whole life, this section is extremely important and close to my heart. Whether you can relate to having these particular insecurities or not, I strongly believe that your health and wellbeing is one of, if not the most important thing to look after at all times.

Growing up working with computers and 9-5 jobs, I have always been cautious of how much time I get in the day to focus on my health and fitness. When you're in a good place both physically and mentally, you are 100 times more likely to be productive and successful. However, when you're trying to make a go of a new business and are putting all your time and effort into making that business a success, it can be easy to overlook your own health and fitness, because you are so focused and may not think you have the time to sleep or exercise or eat healthily. I want to make it clear to you that you DO have time to look after yourself. You ARE allowed to cut out time in your busy day to make sure you are the happiest and healthiest version of yourself. In this chapter I am going to explain my methods of keeping my fitness levels up and how I keep a positive mindset which reflects on the results of my business.

I was always 'the shy one' in school. I was never one to put my hand up or speak up in class and the thought of doing any sort of speaking or presenting physically made me want to cry. This led to major issues with self-confidence and pride as I grew up, from my perception of the way I looked, to my perception of what others thought about me, and it wasn't until half way through my final year of university that I gave myself a stern talking to, which suddenly made everything click for me. You may read this and think it's ridiculous, because I also now think it's ridiculous, but when I first received my overall results from university, a 2:1, I was gutted. I sulked for a good few days because I believed that a 2:1 was not good enough. However, a 2:1 is brilliant and is definitely not something to be ashamed of, and all it took was me reminding my brain of that. My point is, you will not always get the grades you want, and you won't always win the sales that you worked hard for, but that doesn't make you a bad businessperson and it certainly doesn't make you a bad designer. You need to focus on creating a positive mindset which will ultimately lead to your success, both in business and in life.

I remember one of many similar conversations that I had with one of my best friends from university, and whether or not you can relate to this exact scenario, I'm sure there have been times when you have felt stuck, annoyed, stressed because something hasn't gone as smoothly as you may have hoped. During this conversation with my friend I was explaining how I had lost the entirety of my third-year work just weeks before my deadlines due to technical failures on my laptop. At that point I was expecting sympathy, but instead she turned around and basically told me to get over myself. She reminded me that what is done is done, you cannot change what has already happened, but you can change what happens in the future, you can ALWAYS find a positive in what seems to be a negative situation. For example, the negative may have been that I had lost all of my work, but the positives that came from it were me learning to create a high quality body of work to a tight deadline (which is a key skill you will need when working as any type of designer). It wasn't ideal, but I got the work done in time and to a high enough standard to receive a decent grade.

This episode also taught me about the importance of backing up work, ideally in multiple places. Regardless of the size of the job, if something goes wrong and you lose your work, you will have to waste time redoing it – time which you would have been able to put towards another job. It may seem obvious, but I cannot stress enough how important it is to back up your work in more than one place. You may have your own places to save and back up your work, but for me, Google Drive® is a life saver, as it is online and can be accessed from any computer and so can never really be lost. Even if you don't choose to use Google Drive®, I highly recommend using some sort of reliable online backup system so that the work can always be found.

Finally, the biggest positive (to me) that came out of this situation, was realising the amount of support I had from the people around me, particularly my tutor at the time. I was able to tell him everything that had happened, and he was there as someone who understood the pressure of the workload and was aware of the progress I had been making up until that point. He was able to calm me down and reassure me that I would be ok – and I was! The point I am making here is, you cannot do everything on your own. It's taken me a while to realise this but asking for help and leaning on people is definitely NOT a sign of weakness, but a sign of extreme strength. Whether it's a college/university tutor, a family member or a friend, you need someone to keep feeding you that support and motivation, because without it you may lead yourself to believe that you cannot do the things you are on this planet to do, which is ridiculous!

Having a good relationship with my tutor ensured that I had someone to lean on, someone who understood the graphics industry, who knew how to push me to greater success. So, if you have that, then great! If you don't, then it doesn't matter, like I said, it can be anyone you feel comfortable with expressing your feelings and worries to. You may even see myself as that person who is motivating you right now, because I can relate, and the aim of this book is to help you in whichever ways I can.

You will undoubtably get clients who will question your ability to do something, and this may make you briefly question it too, and if you are genuinely worried that you are in over your head, DO NOT PANIC. Take a break, go for a walk, outsource the work. Just find something to take your mind off the stress for a while. Just remember, no setback is too big to risk losing your positive mindset.

I imagine that if you have taken the leap to start up your own Graphic Design business, then you already have the confidence in your ability to make a success out of what you love doing, and I strongly congratulate you for taking this big step. However, if you are like me and sometimes struggle with self-confidence, then the main piece of advice I can give you is to take some time out to reflect and figure out exactly what it is that is hindering your confidence. As soon as you can pinpoint what is preventing you from feeling confident in yourself, you can work on removing or changing that hinderance for your own happiness and wellbeing, and once you do this, you really are unstoppable.

Going back to the brief point I made at the beginning of this section about being too shy to do any type of public speaking or presenting. This was apparent for my entire childhood and at times is still the case today. It was never just a case of nerves, we all get nervous, however this was a case of fearing that the worst would happen, fearing that I wasn't good enough or that people would laugh at me or not take me seriously. This was a serious issue for me that held me back from a lot of experiences.

Luckily, when I started university, there was no space for shyness on my course. I was in amongst some of the most talented and confident people I have ever met in my life – both students and tutors. The tutors ensured that everyone had the same opportunities and really pushed us out of our comfort zones, there was nowhere to hide and at the time I cursed them for it, but I now look back in amazement. During university I found myself putting myself forward for presentations, panels, discussions... everything I was always too shy to even consider in school. Putting myself forward for these things gave me the opportunity to meet some incredible people and visit agencies and places I never would have dreamed of.

Having gone through all of this, I now fully understand why having a voice is so important, especially in this industry where you are constantly required to meet people, talk to people, present your ideas and most importantly, convince everyone that you are the real deal – because you are! Take a leap of faith, sign yourself up for some public speaking or even just start creating content videos of yourself speaking about what you love for social media, you'll be amazed with how good you feel afterwards.

I am not for one second saying that I am a professional mindset or wellbeing coach, however I do see myself as someone who has been in this situation first-hand and has figured all of this stuff out the long and difficult way. So, I would like to offer you the chance of getting in contact with me with any questions or worries you may have on how to help you find your confidence and positive mindset, or even just general advice about your graphic design business. My contact details can be found on my website or at the back of this book. Do not ever be too shy to ask for help if you are struggling.

www.kardesign.org

Healthy Body, Healthy Mind

I have always been focused on keeping fit and active and trying not to let the bad habits and 'cheat days' take control, which has involved being a member of various gyms, downloading mobile apps to track my fitness and buying expensive gadgets to keep me on the move as much as possible. Whether or not you do any of the above, it is still important to take that time out to exercise and keep your body happy and healthy. You don't have to be a marathon runner in your spare time, but you need to know when it's time to take a break from the computer and allow your body to breathe and wind down, and this is how.

It is recommended that you do at least 45 minutes of exercise three times a week, as well as a minimum of 10,000 steps a day. This may sound daunting, especially when you're working 8+ hours a day at a computer and don't seem to have time to spare. It is also recommended that when working a desk-based job it is important to take short but regular breaks. It helps massively if you plan out your days each week so that you know exactly what project you're working on each day, when your deadline is and how long it is likely to take you to complete the project. I tend to keep a physical weekly diary amongst the endless pile of notebooks on my desk, that way I can sit down on a Sunday evening and physically plan out my week, writing down exactly what I'm going to be working on each day and my timings. The point of this is obviously so that you can keep track of your work, but also so you can keep track of your rest. Take a look at my own, simple daily plain, which you can use and adapt for yourself.

	MONDAY	TUESDAY	WEDNESDAY	THURSDAY	FRIDAY	SATURDAY	SUNDAY
8AM							
9AM			Get up, have breakfast, go for a short walk with the dogs				
10AM							
11AM	Work at computer			Work at computer		Work at computer	
12AM		Work at computer					
1PM	Have lunch and go for another walk		Work at computer		Work at computer		
2PM				Have lunch and go for another walk			REST DAY - Take the day to relax and do what YOU want to do
3PM		Go for a walk					
4PM	Work at computer					Take the rest of the day to exercise, shop, socialise - whatever makes you happy	
5PM		Work at computer	Go for a walk/ complete a workout	Work at computer			
6PM	Complete a workout						
7PM					Relax		
8PM		Relax					
9PM	Relax		Relax	Relax			
10PM							

As you can see by my example, no two days are the same. This is done purposely in order to keep your mind engaged. You will also see that I have factored in a big chunk of 'relax' time. It is so important to take the time to relax whenever you can. Fill your day with a busy schedule, have a good amount of sleep and be ready to face the next day with plenty of energy and exciting ideas for your clients.

The beauty of working for yourself is that you can choose your own hours and work around your own schedule, even more reason why you can always make time for your health and wellbeing...no excuses!

I believe that if you can work an exercise routine into your working day, you will not only feel great for doing it, but the work and ideas you produce during those working hours will be presented with a lot more confidence and assurance, which your clients will notice.

I mentioned previously about buying expensive gadgets to help track your fitness. Now, I'm not necessarily saying go and spend hundreds on a brand-new Apple Watch like I did, however since buying my Apple Watch back in 2018, I have been so much more aware of the time I spend not on my feet (maybe at one point, too aware!) This is because, much like many other physical fitness trackers, the Apple Watch has built in features that send you physical reminders to stand up and move around every hour. It also counts your steps, calories and minutes spent exercising, which is a big motivation system to have on your wrist.

There are lots of gadgets out there both expensive and not so expensive that all track relatively similar things from your body, and if you are someone that struggles to find the motivation to exercise, then maybe buying one is a good move for you. This way, your daily results are tracked and stored. This may be a good way of pushing you to take regular breaks from your computer to keep yourself and the watch happy, because at the end of the day, no one wants to waste their time or their money!

Nutrition Is Key

This now takes me on to the dietary aspect of your health and fitness. Diet and fitness go hand in hand for a healthy lifestyle, and so it is equally important to make sure you avoid the tasty sugary temptations that often go with working at a desk all day every day!

If you have ever worked in an office environment, I'm sure you are aware of the struggle to keep a healthy diet when you're working 9-5 (at least!) every day and not having the time or patience to keep an eye on what you're eating during the day. I always find that within office environments, I quickly slip into getting cheap, unhealthy meal-deals for lunch as they are easy and care-free. I would then return to the office after my lunch break to find the dreaded 'cake table' filled with all my favourites to keep the staff happy and motivated to carry on working. Relatable? Maybe.

To avoid these bad eating habits, I would suggest (much like the daily planner I mentioned previously) creating some sort of eating plan. You can do this in any way you feel comfortable with, it doesn't have to be anything extreme, but maybe just something to keep you aware of what you are eating to ensure you remain healthy and balanced, as this will also affect your productivity and energy levels.

This plan could be as simple as keeping a fruit bowl close to your work area and avoiding buying the tempting sweets. One of my weaknesses is, as I work from home, having easy access to the kitchen. When I'm taking a break, it is far too easy to go and binge on whatever is available. But if you limit what is available to you, then you won't have that unhealthy temptation. If the fruit bowl technique doesn't work for you, then maybe adjust your working environment. Take your laptop and some healthy snacks to a library or a park and leave your wallet at home – that way you are unable to buy any food whilst you are out!

Finally, the biggest test on productivity that I have personally tested, is the amount of alcohol you consume. Now, I enjoy a cider as much as the next person, and that is not a bad thing, as long as it's in moderation. However, there was a time during my final year of university where I decided that I was going to take my health and fitness a whole lot more seriously. My main motivation for this was wanting a good final grade, as well as a healthy body. During this time, I decided to cut out alcohol altogether. I got the idea to do this from my mum, who had previously done the same thing for 6 months, and after seeing the incredibly positive affects it had on her health, happiness and productivity, I was excited to see how it would affect me by doing the same thing.

I honestly thought that cutting out alcohol was going to be almost impossible, but in all honesty, it was one of the easiest lifestyle changes I have ever made, and although I only made this change for a few months, the affects it had on me were amazing. During this period of being completely sober, I found myself going to bed earlier, waking up earlier (and completely fresh-headed), and so having a lot more time and energy in my day to get to the gym, enjoy the fresh air and get a full day's work done. The thing I noticed the most was my ability to generate ideas for projects and be productive. Now, this is not a proven scientific fact that cutting out alcohol improves your sense of ideation; however, I strongly believe that it does.

When I decided to start drinking again I also made the decision to still massively reduce the amount I drank, this has meant limiting drinking to weekends, where I knew I had done a productive week's work and so could relax and enjoy myself with a couple of gin and tonics on a Saturday night. I am not telling you that you should do exactly what I did here and that you will only succeed if you don't drink alcohol, however I am saying that being aware of your limits and making healthy decisions that will not only affect your body in a positive way, but also your business, will not do you ANY harm.

I don't want you to think that I am a personal trainer, health coach or nutritionist by any means, but health and fitness has been a passion of mine for many years and I have dedicated a lot of time to learning what is good for the body. I hope you put your trust in me when I say that everything I have written is from either personal experience and thorough research, and I urge you to believe that when you find a healthy routine that works for you, it will make a world of difference for your business, along with your own happiness.

Finally, to summarise, the most important points I would like you to take from this section are:

- **If you feel like the workload is getting too much and you are unable to deal with the stress, take some time to clear your head as NO job is more important than your own wellbeing;**
- **Plan each day, I recommend doing this in a written form either on your computer or in a notebook. This will motivate you to stick to it and be productive each day;**
- **When planning your day, try and avoid too much of a solid routine, alter the number of hours you spend working each day to keep your brain alert;**
- **Dedicate a generous amount of time to exercise each week, the average is around 45 minutes of exercise 3 times a week, as well as at least 10,000 steps a day;**
- **Be kind to your body, eat well, get plenty of sleep and try and resist those naughty habits;**
- **Rely on the close people around you for when you are struggling, do NOT ever suffer in silence.**

SECTION 3
OUTSOURCING

Outsourcing is one of the single most helpful things anyone can do for themselves and others in business. Outsourcing basically means giving aspects of your workload to other people instead of doing it yourself. People generally outsource work for reasons such as not having the specific knowledge, equipment or software to complete a certain job or maybe just lack of time, and there is no shame in having any of these reasons. The biggest example I can give based on my own personal experience is clients wanting web design. When wanting a new website, most clients will expect everything to be included, from the overall design, to the hosting, and if you are like me, you may not have skills/interest in the hosting aspect of websites, which is where outsourcers who specialise in web hosting come in. That way I don't have to let the client down and the outsourcer also gets business...win-win!

If you are unsure about where to find outsourcers, there are many websites in which you can find people for all sorts of projects, some examples are www.upwork.com, www.fiverr.com and www.freelancer.com, which I will cover more thoroughly throughout the chapter.

If you are new to all of this and have never posted a job advert before, I recommend you start with making a bulleted list of exactly what you are looking for in an outsourcer, a few examples being:

- **What skills do they need to ensure they complete the task to a high standard?**

- **Will the work they do reflect positively on your business?**

- **Are they good communicators?**

- **Are they trustworthy?**
- **What is their budget?**

In order to ensure you are choosing the right outsourcer for the job, you need to conduct a lot of research into the potential matches.

How To Post A Job Advert

Upwork is a widely used and extremely highly regarded, global freelancing platform that has been built to make your life easier! How Upwork functions is the client in search of a freelancer will post a job advert for potential freelancers to bid on. Alternatively, you can search for your own freelancer.

The Upwork homepage is conveniently separated into sections to make your quest easier for you. These categories include Web, Mobile & Software Development, Design & Creative, Writing, Sales & Marketing and more...

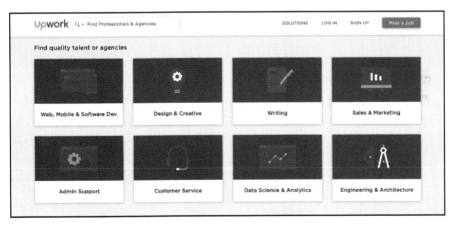

Let's say you are looking for a photographer to take some product shots for a marketing campaign requested by one of your clients. You will begin by clicking the 'Design & Creative' category on the homepage, you will then select 'Photography'. Upwork then asks you what the estimated scope of the work will be, and for this example I will say it is short term work that will last for less than a month.

The next step is very important, and you need to consider a few things whilst making the choice of experience level required. Factors to consider are:

- **The size and scope of your client's project;**
- **The likelihood of you needing further work of this freelancer in the future;**
- **Your own budget.**

Within my example I am going to say that my client is a start-up business in a very small, local area. They are looking to kick start their new brand with a fun advertising campaign to let their audience know who they are and what they're about. Due to the small, local nature of this start up, their budget is relatively low, and they do not yet have the finances to spend a lot of money on this one aspect of the brand.

However, as they are wanting this campaign to be the launch of their brand to the public, it needs to be professional and extremely eye catching, and so potentially requires more than an entry level photographer. It is highly likely that an expert photographer will charge a lot more than an entry level photographer, which will obviously affect the amount you charge to your client. Therefore, in this scenario, the most reasonable option would be to go for an intermediate photographer. This means that there is also potential for you and this freelancer to continue to work and grow together without the prices being too high or too low.

I think it is extremely helpful to find yourself a network of free-lancers who you use repeatedly as opposed to hiring a new one for each project. This will also give your own business and portfolio a consistent look, which will make you more desirable to potential future clients. This also allows you to build a good relationship with these freelancers and develop mutual trust and understanding of the way you both run your businesses.

On the other hand, not all may be how they appear, and you need to know how to spot the red flags and how to avoid working with someone who may take advantage or may not be the right person for the job.

As I mentioned before, you need to do your research beforehand and you need to pinpoint the exact characteristics, skills, expe-rience and price range that you are looking for in a freelancer, and you need to settle for nothing less than exactly what you are looking for. For example, you may find that you are more willing to put your trust in someone that is slightly more experienced and has been doing the job for longer, and so you need to pay attention to the number of hours the freelancer has worked, which can be viewed on the freelancer's profile. Whilst looking at this, you also need to consider whether this freelancer is working too many hours and so may not be able to reliably commit to your timeframes. However, only you can decide whether or not specific freelancers meet your specific requirements, as every project and every person is different. You also need to keep in mind that these freelancers are doing the same research on who they want as a client and could easily be researching how to take advantage of start-ups like yourself.

One example situation could be that you find a freelancer on Upwork who seems to tick all the boxes, has enough experience to understand and take on the job and whose price is within your budget. This sounds perfect but let me remind you of a point I made previously about having contracts signed and in place before any work is started. This will cover both yours, and the freelancer's back in any case of a problem.

As a businessowner yourself, and as someone who is new to the business industry, it is inevitable that your prices will start out relatively low so that you can attract those initial clients. It is also inevitable that as you become more established, your prices will increase due to your increase in skills, knowledge and clients – and rightly so! However, this is something you need to take into consideration whilst hiring an outsourcer. Much like yourself, they may be relatively new to the industry and so have relatively low prices. Initially, you may think this is great and jump at this opportunity, but do not forget that it is likely that over time, these prices will most likely increase and if you are not careful and do not establish that loyalty and a set price at the beginning, you may be ripped off further down the line. This would mean you would also have to up your own prices to be able to make the job worthwhile, which could potentially upset your relationships with your own clients.

Along with the price increase, you could also find that over time, the freelancer extends their deadlines and begins to prioritise other clients over you, and you may be left paying really high prices for unrealistically long turnaround times, which is not ideal for anyone. So, like I keep reiterating, write up a contract and set your terms from the beginning!

To summarise and conclude this theoretical situation, there is an option for you to view the success ratings of each freelancer on Upwork, which will allow you to find the best person for the job based on their reviews from previous clients, which can all be viewed at the bottom of the freelancer's profile. Remember the emphasis I put on reviews in chapter one – the attention you pay to the reviews on the freelancer's profiles is the same attention your clients will pay to your own reviews and the more positive reviews, the more likely it is that the job will go to that person!

How To Advertise Yourself As An Outsourcer

There may come a time where you are at a loose end and wondering what to do to get work – trust me, I have been there plenty of times! Maybe it's getting towards the end of the year and there is not much demand for graphic design in your circle. What I recommend doing in this case, is to advertise yourself as an outsourcer on these websites. This will keep up your chances of getting new clients and even expand your network of connections in the big world of designers, which is incredibly important.

Much like before, I will use Upwork as my example. However, these steps can be used and applied to pretty much any form of outsourcer advertising, both on and offline.

First and foremost, you need to be completely honest with your potential clients when advertising yourself as a freelancer. There is no gain in pretending to be something you're not just for the sake of looking more experienced than you potentially are right now.

On Upwork, the best chance you have at getting yourself noticed as a freelancer, is by having a stand-out profile. You can personalise your profile by going to settings in the top right-hand corner of the screen and clicking 'my profile', the rest is self-explanatory. You can see examples from my specialised profile in the screenshot below. This should help you understand what is required in order to get that work!

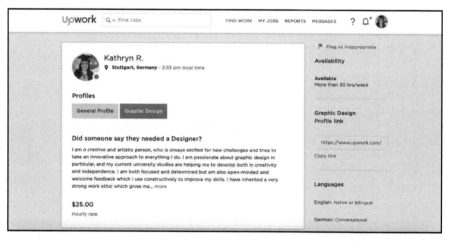

When advertising yourself, always commit a lot of time to your introduction, your biography...the small piece of writing that could be the deciding factor over whether you get that job or not.

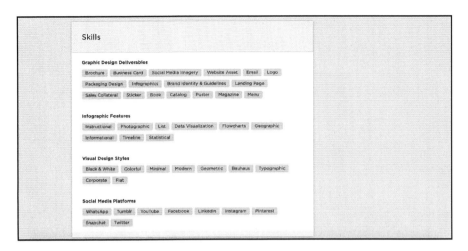

Much like when writing a personal statement or a CV, you need to highlight your skills and your passions in a short and snappy way so that the reader doesn't get bored but gets more and more intrigued and impressed. Like I have in my introduction on Upwork, open your statement with a clean sentence that literally describes your abilities and why you have chosen this path. The rest of the content should then flow naturally as you are clearly passionate about design and are keen on getting that work.

When advertising on other platforms such as Facebook, LinkedIn, Twitter etc. I always recommend adding a link to your website or portfolio, as this is a quick and easy way for the potential client to view your work without having to work hard to find it. Always have it handy, as you never know who is looking at your portfolio and you absolutely never know who you are going to meet on a day to day basis.

Which Websites Work Best?

As you can probably assume, for me, Upwork is the ideal platform for finding a high quality, reliable and experienced freelancer. However, Upwork is just one of many online platforms where you can find freelancers.

Another great example is Fiverr.com. Fiverr is much like Upwork in terms of how it works and the results you get, however it is definitely the cheaper alternative, as you are able to get every job done for just $5! There is no doubt that if you are looking for an extremely cost-effective service, that Fiverr.com is the go-to website, as the quality of work is overall very good.

Though you might be thinking, "high quality work for just $5? What could go wrong? Why would I use any other platform?", much like every platform out there, Fiverr has its downsides.

Though Fiverr is so amazingly cheap, the downside is that it is also highly popular due to the low prices. This means that the freelancers may be snowed under with commissions, making the deadlines unrealistic and long-winded. If you require a fast service, of course you will need to pay more for the privilege. Due to the vast number of buyers and the unrealistic deadlines, this could result in rushed, lower quality outcomes which is something you need to consider whilst choosing your platform.

Overall, I highly recommend using a platform such as Fiverr for quick and simple projects, projects that don't require a lot of complicated technical aspects. I also recommend that, if you plan on using Fiverr to find an outsourcer, always ensure that you ask for any source files and ALL assets used for this project that the freelancer has had access to, this avoids any complications or the misplacing of files later on, which is easily done!

Finally, much like any other outsourcing platform, make sure that communication with freelancers on Fiverr is effective and consistent from both ends during the completion of the project. It could be that if you aren't proactive with your communication, the freelancer could unknowingly put other, more proactive clients before you, and your project could be delayed or lost, which isn't good for anyone! Make sure you keep each other in the loop at all times and ensure that the freelancer is honest, reliable and respectful of your time and money.

Another alternative would be to find work through social media. Now, I would not usually recommend doing this as a first resort, as you are way more likely to secure a genuine and reliable freelancer through a website tailored to making that happen. However, social media platforms such as Facebook and LinkedIn are constantly being updated with new professional tools to help your business and to help you network. I will go more into the advertising side of it in section four, but for now I will focus solely on hiring freelancers.

For myself, Facebook has been a brilliant platform that has allowed me to not only showcase my work, but also get work. I was in contact with a lady who posted an advert on a Facebook Conversation Group based around where I come from in Somerset, who was after a graphic designer to update her website for her. All it took was a few simple messages back and forth and a link to see the website she wanted updating and we had a deal. Like I said, this is not my number one recommended way of finding work, and there is every chance you could be scammed as Facebook is not specifically intended as an outsourcing website. However, there is always a chance of finding reasonably priced work on Facebook if, like I said before, you do all of you research BEFORE signing any contracts!

If you are planning on searching for work on Facebook, I strongly recommend creating a business page first. This will give you a platform where you can instantly show your potential clients that you are serious, and they are also able to view any posts and reviews left on your page – back to the importance of getting reviews and making your online presence known! I will cover how to create an effective and professional-looking Facebook business page in section four.

There are hundreds of outsourcing websites out there, I have just named a few. It is extremely important to conduct thorough research into each of these websites, be it Upwork.com, Fiverr. com, Freelancer.com or even social media platforms such as Facebook and LinkedIn. If you are sensible and know exactly who you are looking for to get the job done correctly, you should not have a problem. Take your time when doing this research as it is way more important to find the right freelancer on the right website over a longer period of time, than to just settle for the first person that responds to your advert.

SECTION 4
SOCIAL MEDIA

Every year social media platforms are evolving and becoming more and more widely used by the general population, and because of this, it is an extremely good tool that you should always use to your business' advantage.

When advertising yourself, there are a lot of things you need to consider to ensure that you turn those potential clients into definite clients! I highly recommend making a list, or some sort of spreadsheet or document, in which you write down all the important things you want your client to know about your business at a first glance. As I mentioned before, it is always useful to keep a notebook handy wherever you go, because you never know where and when you will find inspiration or think of a new and creative way to advertise yourself.

Facebook

I want to begin this section with Facebook, one of the largest and most widely used social media platform in the world, and whether you love it or hate it, we can't deny that it is a powerful platform with so many different uses, the main one (for the purpose of this book) being having and building your professional presence.

I'm pretty sure that Facebook was the first platform I went to when I first started KARD Graphic Design and to be honest, I had no idea how to use it to my business' advantage, I just felt like I needed to have a professional Facebook page because everyone else did.

For the first 6-7 months of KARD Graphic Design's appearance on Facebook, the account may as well have been inactive, as all I did was invite the people on my friends list to like the page and post the occasional throwback picture to a piece of work I did a year or so prior. I then finally decided that it was time to start making the most of this amazing platform and start getting some work from it.

If you haven't already made one, I suggest you create yourself a business page on Facebook, and if you don't use Facebook, that's fine, however for the purpose of your business I strongly recommend making an account purely for your business. You can see mine in the image below.

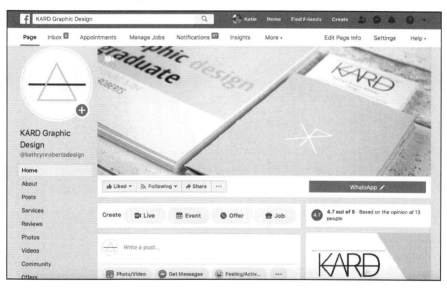

When creating your business page, you need to ensure that you fill out all of the relevant information in the 'About' section, as this is what your clients will be interested in reading. What I also suggest is keeping this information short, sweet, and to the point. This is Facebook after all, and so I would use this as a way of adding a more friendly and casual tone to your page whilst still highlighting that you are a serious business. You can use my 'About' page from KARD Graphic Design as an example and template wherein you can develop your own page.

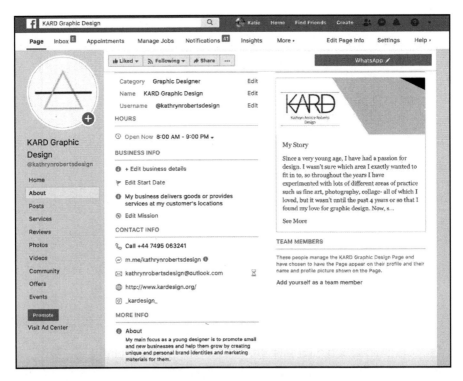

Once you have your page set up, it is then very important to ensure it is kept active and up to date. You should be regularly posting content, be it old work, recent work, stuff shared from other people or just text posts to let your audience know that you are an active business.

This takes me on to the content aspect. It's easy for me to tell you to keep your Facebook Business page up to date with lots of enticing posts, but you're probably now sat there wondering what on earth you need to be posting to attract that audience.

Firstly, I believe that your page should be an even mixture of different types of content, meaning posts where you are showing off a personal project you completed in your own time, to creating promotions, competitions and adverts, to posting examples of work that you've done for your clients in order to not only advertise yourself, but to advertise them – most clients really appreciate this.

Below is an example of a personal post on my Facebook page. This was showing images of design-related stuff that I have found whilst out and about. I believe that actively sharing posts like this allows your audience to see your true passion for design, and that your passion is a hobby as well as a business. This will help people trust your ability to produce genuine, heartfelt work for them and it will also show them that you are not just in it for the money.

My next example is a post showing some client work. This was a client I have been working with from the beginning of their journey and so I was extremely keen to help promote their brand as well as my own, and if you look at my page, you will see that I am regularly resharing posts from this client, a charity with an extremely touching story and motive that I highly recommend you check out! This post not only includes graphic design work from myself, but also examples of studio photography that I do to present my work.

This leads me to a very important point I want to make about the presentation of your online posts. As you can see in the above example, I have taken the time to produce high quality photographs in order to ensure that the post is presented in a professional manner, this not only makes my page stand out and look good, but it also gives the client a look of professionalism and class. I urge you to take the time to photograph your products properly, it doesn't necessarily mean that you should go out and by the newest camera and studio lighting, a lot of my photographs have been taken on my iPhone, but just ensure that you give a generous amount of time to making your posts look as professional as possible.

My final Facebook post example is a paid promotion. To me, the best ways to catch the eye of a potential client is to use an image that stands out but also represents your abilities to a high standard, and to also keep the information as short and to the point as possible, so that the person reading it doesn't get bored and move on. What also works is having a key statement or offer on the first line to entice your client and make them want to keep reading. Below is an example Facebook advert posted from my KARD Graphic Design page. I used my birthday month as an excuse to put an offer out on Facebook to make my potential clients feel involved and like they were also being gifted for my birthday. This landed me one of my first long term clients, who is regularly in contact for more design work.

KARD Graphic Design is 🎉 celebrating July.

July 2, 2018 · 🌐

HAPPY BIRTHDAY TO KATHRYN!

As July is filled with so many important birthdays in my life, including my 21st, I want you to celebrate with me by giving your business and clients a unique new logo, 250 double sided, fully coloured business cards and 50 single sided, fully coloured A5 flyers for just £90 instead of the usual price of £140!

Offer available until 31st July 2018. Contact me now to discuss this limited time offer further!

I would like to suggest things to bear in mind and try to avoid if you are going to go down the route of paid Facebook adverts. When I first discovered Facebook for business and the wonderful and interesting world of paying to advertise on Facebook, I can honestly say that I got extremely carried away with the excitement of paying such small amounts of money to receive hundreds of page likes and the odd commission.

The way Facebook adverts work is that you set yourself a daily budget and intended radius in which you wish to gain audience attention. This budget can be as low as 50p a day, which I thought was incredible, as this 50p a day resulted in me gaining lots of recognition from people outside of my network. However, for me, this 50p a day soon turned into £5 a day and so on, which resulted in me spending a big chunk of my earnings on realistically nothing but page likes. This meant that at the end of my first financial year, I made a loss due to the sheer amount of money I spent on Facebook compared to the money I was earning.

I'm not saying that Facebook adverts do not work, as regardless of how much money I spent on them, I still managed to get work and I highly support that Facebook is an extremely powerful and positive platform that will help you if you follow the correct procedures. The reason I had this unsuccessful experience with Facebook at the beginning was purely because I was so new to it and did not do my research first and I had no idea of how to spend my business money wisely.

When establishing your business on Facebook and making your start in the incredible world of Facebook advertising, just don't fall into the same addicted spiral that I did, choose your budget wisely and make sure your content is relevant enough to attract the attention you want it to get and make sure that you calculate your finances prior to setting up any Facebook promotions, make sure you have enough money in your budget to ensure this doesn't result in a loss, like it did with me.

When creating a promoted advert, I recommend using a similar type style to the one I used in my previous example. The key points to have in mind when writing your content are:

- **Begin with a short, eye-catching question, statement or offer to draw in your potential client's attention. For example: 'Only 7 Days before this special offer ends!' 'Nothing says summer like a £50 discount! If you like the sound of this, keep reading!'**

- **Ask rhetorical questions to get people thinking: 'Are you a business start-up looking to increase your client basis and recognition?'**

- **Use bullet points instead of paragraphs to highlight your key points. If you fill your advert with too much block text, the chances are that people will keep scrolling past it – let's face it, we're all guilty of doing this!**

Bear in mind, that this information I am giving you about advertising yourself can be adapted and used in many different ways both on and offline. We are graphic designers after all, the world of graphics and advertising is our oyster, so embrace it and enjoy it!

Instagram

Following on from this, I want to touch on Instagram. Personally, I use my professional Facebook and Instagram accounts hand in hand. This means that 9 times out of 10, whatever is posted on one account, is automatically posted to the other one too.

I personally do not use Instagram to necessarily get clients and aggressively advertise, because to me, Instagram was not made for this. I use it more for what I believe the platform is originally intended for, which is to blog. What I like about Instagram is the effect of the hashtag system, which can be used to your business' advantage to gain recognition. I keep a list of relevant hashtags saved in the notes section on my phone, so that when I go to post something on Instagram, I already have a series of hashtags that I can copy and paste onto the post to save me having to rewrite them every time. Of course, each post is different and so requires different text and different hashtags to make it relevant, but having that standard list saved is a massive timesaver.

Take the example post below, this was a massive commission for me from my university, and I was incredibly proud of it. As you can see, I have put a caption that is personal to me and not trying to obviously advertise my services. However, due to the nature of the post, the advertisement within goes without me needing to spell it out. It is clear that I have completed some paid work for a big client, due to the opening words 'Biggest commission yet', I then go on to show how humble I am to have received this commission, it is so important to stay humble at every point of your career, do not ever let success get to your head, but with this you need to stay proud and show off your skills. You can also see that I have rounded the post up with a series of hashtags that are entirely relevant to the post.

This means that anyone who searches for these hashtags will see this post amongst others who have used the same hashtags, and if your post stands out enough, it could attract the business you want and even the business you don't realise that you want.

Make sure that when you are choosing your hashtags, you make them relevant to what you want people to hire you for, there is no use in putting the hashtag '#webdesigner' if you have no desire to design websites. This may seem obvious, but it is easy to get carried away with hash tagging everything to receive post likes and follows. You don't want to mislead people into thinking you're something that you're not and have no intention of being.

I think that including images of yourself on your social media accounts is also very important, because it allows your audience to put a face to your company name and get to know you as a person as well as a designer. Doing this will also help get your confidence up, as if you currently consider yourself as quite camera shy, gradually putting yourself out there for the world to see will help build up that positive view on yourself. This may start with the odd photo or selfie linked to your work, it may then lead to videos of you talking about your work, to podcasts and interviews and even live panels, the opportunities are endless and all it takes is the building up of your self-confidence as I mentioned back in section two. This will do wonders for your social media presence and the success of your business.

Twitter

I personally do not use Twitter for my business at this moment in time. There is no real reason as to why I don't use it professionally other than simply not yet having the time to devote to it just yet. However, I do fully intend on eventually starting up a Twitter account for KARD Graphic Design, and I have previously used Twitter for my own personal use, so I am extremely aware of its unique and excellent facets that can definitely work to your advantage.

The beauty of Twitter, is that it runs solely on providing content that people can relate to or enjoy enough to want to share on their own profile, and getting your Tweets seen by the world is not as difficult as it may seem, providing you get the content right!

Unlike Facebook, you do not need to rely on paid promotions to get your profile and adverts seen by a large amount of people in a short space of time. On Twitter, all you need to do is Tweet something that your potential clients can relate to enough to make them want to share with the world. This can include promotions, e.g. 'The first 20 people to Retweet and Favourite this tweet will receive 50% off their next order of business cards when purchased from KARD Graphic Design. Check your DM's afterwards to get the full details on how to claim your discount!' – Something as easy as pressing a button is definitely not going to turn people away, and who doesn't love a discount?

Twitter doesn't even have to be about openly advertising your services and pushing promotions to gain attention from the public, it could even just be a case of writing something witty and funny or something that has happened to you that people can relate to and laugh at, something like "surely every designer can relate to this...". Remember, as soon as someone favourites or retweets you, your post will then become available for all of that person's followers, and this is how the chain begins...completely for free!

This can arguably be a no-brainer when it comes to choosing which platforms are best to advertise your business. However, you also need to consider who your target audience is, as it is found that there is a smaller age bracket that use Twitter compared to other social media platforms, and so you may need to work out whether it will be worth devoting your time to Twitter when you are promoting yourself to the wrong age range. This statement applies to all social media platforms, as they all attract many different types of users which could either be beneficial to your personal business, or it may lead to you not gaining the right attention for your intended market.

LinkedIn

The final social media platform I would like to cover, is the extremely powerful and professional tool that is LinkedIn. LinkedIn is reputed to be the world's leading networking site for professionals, students and jobseekers, and this is why making your presence on there is so important, so if you don't have an account already...you really don't know what you're missing, so make one now and get networking!

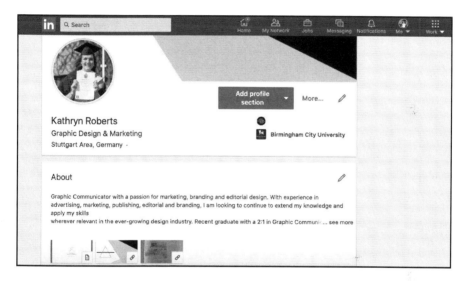

LinkedIn is not only a place to showcase your work and brag about your many skills as a designer, but it's a way for you to recruit clients and advertise your services in arguably, a more professional way than Facebook, Instagram and Twitter. LinkedIn was created to help professionals like yourself meet your potential match in a client or employer.

In my opinion, the most effective way to get noticed by potential clients and also employers/freelancers, is to be active in communication and interaction on the platform. This means following companies and people that take your interest, reaching out to people, commenting and reacting to their LinkedIn posts. One of the many benefits of LinkedIn, is the function that allows you to be notified when someone has viewed your profile. Do not take this as a bad thing, your name popping up in a notification on a potential client/employers account means that they will notice you and potentially look at your account in return – this is the beginning of your networking experience with this person, go with it and make the most of it!

Although LinkedIn is such a successful platform for finding work and making connections, this also means that many other people are using it for the same function. Therefore, the competition is going to be extremely high, and you'll have to put in some extra effort in order to stand out from the crowd.

This takes me back to my point about being active. You don't have to be the best, most qualified designer out there to win the business, because realistically, who decides who is really the best designer? What you DO need to be is persistent and show your passion for the subject and your willingness to work – this is what will win you the sale. Your engagement in the professional lives of these people will stand out much more than shoving work in their faces that may or may not be what they are looking for – this is definitely not to say that you shouldn't proudly show off your achievements, but make it seem like it's under their terms. This is what makes LinkedIn and email advertising different from Facebook advertising. On Facebook, people are not out looking for you, and they are potentially not even looking for anything work-related. You need to catch their attention in a more forceful way by placing adverts containing temptations such as special offers and discounts right in their newsfeed.

When I was in my final year at university, there was one global company that caught my attention. This company had strong links with the university and through that I was able to meet the employees and attend various workshops and events held by this company. Once I got it in my head that I wanted to be a part of this company, being the stubborn and persistent person that I am, I went out of my way to connect on LinkedIn with the people I had met from the company, send private messages and emails to the recruiters and constantly engage with their social media presence.

Doing this meant that these people remembered me and were happy to connect with me, which was great...but for me it wasn't enough, because I didn't just want to connect with them, I wanted to work for them.

A few months went by and during that time I graduated from university, but still had my heart set on this company. Their social media and email replies became shorter and the response time became longer. So, I took it into my own hands and turned up on the company's doorstep with my CV and portfolio. I was serious about getting this work, and this is the enthusiasm you should apply to every single job you face.

Ultimately, circumstances dictated that I was not in a position to work for that company. However, this experience pushed me to go entirely out of my comfort zone and move to Germany for work instead. I see this is an advantage and I also still have the contacts I made from the company for potential opportunities in the future. No book should ever be closed in the world of networking, put in the effort to make these contacts now, because you never know when you will need each other in the future.

How Does Your Website Look?

I want to conclude this section with a small guide on how to optimise your website content in order to get the most out of it as possible.

To begin with, as a designer who is offering a service to the public, it is crucial that you have a website to direct people to when you first meet them or when you're advertising on social media. It's professional and a great way to get your name out there on the world wide web! It is also important that you keep your website as up to date as possible at all times, as you never know who is looking at it at any time.

I created my website on Wix, and if you have ever used Wix before, you will know that it is a pretty straightforward and uncomplicated web design platform to use, which is exactly why I used it. There are plenty of other web design platforms out there that are arguably more challenging, such as Wordpress, Squarespace, Adobe Dreamweaver and many more, but I personally find that for the purpose of my business, Wix was ideal.

Using my website as my example, I want to start by highlighting my domain name 'www.kardesign.org'. As you may know, a domain name is the purchasable address of a website that is unique to that website and company. These can also be used within email addresses to protect businesses and give a professional look and feel.

A domain name can be purchased through various organisations, for example Google, Godaddy and Wix and generally cost around £15-£20/year. I believe that it is extremely important to pay that small amount of money for a unique domain name, as it looks so much more professional than having something that is water-marked, such as kardesign.wixsite.com. Clients will take you a lot more seriously if they can see that you have taken the time and effort to make your website unique to your business. Another piece of advice I'd like to give is that it could be advantageous to your business if you also look into purchasing other domain names that are similar and may appear threatening to yours. This potentially avoids competitors creating websites that may defer the attention from yours.

Now, moving on to the content of your website. I have split it into 5 main sections: Home, Services, Experience, Portfolio and Contact. I have also added an extra section purely dedicated to my university dissertation, this is purely because it's a piece of work that I am proud of and want people to read for the time being, but it's not crucial to have there.

As you can see from the screenshot of my homepage, the general design of the website is extremely simple and clean. You do not want your website to be too overcrowded, as it makes it look claustrophobic and may put your audience off exploring it due to being too overwhelmed with information and content.

Obviously, there are so many different ways that you can express yourself on your website, and I always think it's a good idea to take inspiration from other design-based websites. I have chosen to use my website as more of a portfolio/CV platform to keep my proudest, most up to date work all in one place, so that any potential employers, employees or clients can see it conveniently at any time.

Make sure that your website is easy to navigate, make sure all buttons are clearly marked and that there is no way that a visitor can miss something that you intend for them to see. I also recommend keeping the word content minimal. We are designers, and so our potential clients will be expecting to see visual representations of our talents, not pages upon pages of text. On my website homepage, I have included a short biography to introduce myself to the viewer, along with a relevant and up to date photograph of myself. This allows the visitor to get a sense of who I am as a person and designer without having to look too far. If you're going to do this, I recommend writing 3-4 sentences at most to keep the visitor interested in finding out more. Paying close attention to the content written on your website is what creates traffic for the site, also known as website visitors. This process is called Search Engine Optimisation (SEO), this works through focusing on which words people are searching for on search engines such as Google. Again, you need to do your research in advance to figure out the statistics around SEO for your particular website to find out the best ways to optimise your content and get the most website views you possibly can.

As you can see in the below screenshot, in the 'Experience' section of my website, I have created a timeline of my previous work experience. This allows me to include lots of content without going overboard on the text, as a timeline needs to be concise. You can also include imagery to reduce the amount of text even more. I believe timelines are a great way of showing your experience in a fun yet professional manner.

My final tip for your website is to ensure that it contains links to take your clients to your social media platforms. This is something that many people look out for on websites for various reasons, such as finding reviews on your business, seeing your general tone and seeing how up to date you are with the design industry. This takes me back to the importance of being active on social media. You want your clients to see that you are passionate about your subject and also up to date with the latest in the design industry – this is super attractive to potential clients.

SECTION 5
MARKETING & BUSINESS

Personally, one of the main reasons I chose to take the plunge and start up my own business, was not only my passion for graphic design, but my extreme interest and fascination in the marketing and business side of it. I absolutely love networking, meeting new people and talking about business and how I can possibly help people.

You may be in the same position as me and have an interest in business and marketing, and if so then that is a great start into the world of running your own business. If not, then that is not a problem! It has been said many times that you do not need to know about business to run a business. However, I strongly believe that having some idea and even the slightest bit of interest in business will always give you a boost.

As you progress over time, you will naturally pick up more tips on how to run your business and eventually it will become a second nature to you. As I mentioned previously, you clearly carry the confidence and motivation to make your business work and you are clearly passionate about design. However, as you are at the beginning of your journey, let me teach you my ways.

Establishing Your Target Audience

Knowing your target audience inside and out is a vital component to running your business smoothly and successfully, and this is one thing that I got very wrong when I started out with my business, and it unfortunately cost me dearly.

When I first started KARD Graphic Design, I was so wrapped up in the excitement of it all, that I just wanted to design stuff for EVERYONE, and this is what I attempted to market towards.

However, I soon learnt the hard way that this was not the correct way to get clients, it actually had the opposite affect and I received next to no clients as my marketing was too broad and not specific enough to attract the attention I needed.

Imagine you are on a fishing boat in the middle of the Bristol Channel, you know that there are thousands of species of fish below you, however none of them take even the slightest bit of interest in your fishing line. This is because you have attached bait that attracts freshwater fish yet are fishing in saltwater. This doesn't mean you have not attached bait to your fishing line, it just means that the bait you are using is not targeting the fish that you are after. You may be thinking, what on earth has fishing got to do with me finding clients for my graphic design business?

Your marketing is your bait, the more research you do into your chosen fish species (or target audience) and the more specific you are with your marketing, the more likely you are to catch the fish (and get the business you want!)

How do you narrow down your target audience? Well, I strongly suggest (much like most other research tasks) starting with a pen and a sheet of paper with the words 'Target Audience' circled in the middle.

Begin by jotting down keywords/headings that will help you pinpoint your target audience:

- **Age;**
- **Gender;**
- **Location;**
- **Demographic.**

and so on...

Then you literally just need to write words under these headings of the type of client that:

A. Appeals to you personally

and

B. Appeals to the services you are offering

When completing this task, there are key questions you need to ask yourself in order to make sure you are marketing to the right people, these questions include:

- **Am I aiming at start-up businesses like myself?**
- **Am I aiming at established businesses?**
- **Am I aiming at small business, or large?**
- **Am I aiming at young people?**
- **Am I aiming at a particular industry?**
- **Am I aiming at people only in the UK, or Worldwide?**

Figuring out your target audience can be a long and tiring process, but as soon as you do this and create a marketing strategy along with adverts (which I will go through in further detail I section four) to fit this, your dream clients will start lining up and making important decisions for your business will become a lot easier in the future.

Know & Understand Your Intellectual Property

When I was first starting out with KARD Graphic Design, I had no idea about any of this stuff and if you are just starting out then it is highly possible you don't either. It is my aim to explain it all in a way that will help you get your head around it (hopefully) a lot quicker than I did! Knowing your intellectual rights is extremely important and can potentially save your business and your work from being taken advantage of, so I highly recommend that you take the time to learn and understand it to the max.

In 2018, I attended The Business Show for the first time at the ExCel in London. My intention was to do some networking and to find out how I can improve my business along with what important things were missing from my business to hinder my success. I found the show incredibly helpful and eye opening and since then have had the urge to revisit the show every year. Most importantly because it taught me everything I needed to know about intellectual property and trademarks. It also opened my eyes to the wonderful world of book writing after meeting my book mentor Richard McMunn!

You may be reading this already as a registered trademark or limited company, and if this is the case, to start with I highly congratulate you for taking the time and responsibility to get your business registered appropriately. This may also mean that this information may not be as relevant to you as someone who maybe hasn't yet considered becoming a registered trademark or limited company. When I was at The Business Show, I attended a presentation by the Intellectual Property Office (IPO), where I learnt a lot about the major differences between copyright and trademarks and why it is so important to have your business registered as a trademark to avoid any (potentially expensive) problems later on down the line.

In section one I explained the ins and outs of copyright, and how important it is to protect your work until yourself and the client are happy with the work produced and you have received full payment. In this section I will go into more detail about trademarks and whether or not it is necessary to have them.

According to the IPO, a trademark is anything that can be represented graphically, such as a letter, word, name, signature, brand, logo, shape, colour etc. and can be used to distinguish brand identities, goods or services. Unlike copyright, you have to register and pay for a trademark and until you do this, any icon, name or slogan used to represent your brand or services is free for anyone else to use. However, once you have successfully registered for your trademark, it then belongs to you and you then have the right to challenge anyone who uses it for themselves.

The process of registering for a trademark is relatively simple and although it costs money, I personally believe that it is worth every penny! To begin the process, you must first find out if the item you wish to trademark is available - in other words someone else may have had a similar idea to you and got in there first. You can check this and apply for your trademark by visiting https://trademarks.ipo.gov.uk/ipo-apply, here it explains the process step by step in a relatively quick and easy way, so if after reading this section you now feel like you need to get your unique brand trademarked before someone else (legally) claims it for their own, then get it done now!

Please bear in mind that as of the 31st January 2020, the UK has left the EU, this means that during the transition period (1st February 2020 – 31st December 2020) changes are likely to be made regarding the IPO and other important business requirements, so although everything I am saying is completely valid and true, and all UK laws remain the same until the 31st December 2020, I urge you to keep an eye on any updates via www.gov.uk and always be aware of any changes to the system. I don't want your business to suffer due to miscommunication.

VAT...To Register Or Not To Register

The next thing I learnt from The Business Show was about Value Added Tax (VAT) registration. If you are currently running your business as a freelancer and have not yet registered as self-employed, I recommend you do that now. To register yourself as self-employed, you need to visit the 'working for yourself' section on the gov.uk website – please read all the information about self-employment available on the website before taking any action. Doing this will hopefully help you to get a sense of where you are with your business, your profits and losses and whether or not you are eligible to pay tax!

Did you know...for the 2019/20 tax year, if you are self-employed, you can earn up to £12,500 before you need to pay tax? After that, you will need to pay the basic rate of income tax on income up to £50,000 which is 20%. Hopefully this will help you figure out how much tax you should be paying each year – if any! However, the threshold changes from year to year, so you will need to check this figure regularly so that you are always up to date on the tax situation. This brings me on to Value Added Tax (VAT) and the pros and cons of VAT registration.

I want to begin by saying that as of 2019/20, if your VAT taxable turnover exceeds £85,000 then you are required to register for VAT. However, if you are just starting up your business then it is unlikely that you will be turning over this sum right now, and so the choice to become VAT registered remains with you. Let me start with giving some advantages of voluntary VAT registration:

- **You are able to apply VAT to the total costs of your services, increasing your profit;**

- **You are able to claim VAT back on purchases that have gone through your VAT registered business – e.g. if you are paying for printing, you will be able to claim the VAT back from the total cost of printing;**

- **Being VAT registered arguably makes your business more attractive to other businesses, it makes you look more established and it makes you look like you know your stuff when it comes to business, which could just land you some more clients!**

These advantages may have already made your mind up about becoming VAT registered, however there are also some disadvantages that you need to also consider:

- **Adding VAT to your services will make your services more expensive overall, which may be advantageous to you, however not so advantageous to your theoretical non-VAT registered client, who is not keen on paying the extra amount as they cannot claim it back;**

- **You are expected to keep every VAT invoice and receipt and being VAT registered undoubtably means MORE paperwork, which if you're like me, is a nightmare!**

You can register for VAT by visiting www.gov.uk and following the links and instructions relevant to 'Money and tax'. The gov. uk website is an extremely useful tool that will help you in pretty much all aspects of running your business, as well as general and important life-related things including important travel documents, housing and childcare. So, if you don't already, I recommend you create an account and familiarise yourself with the website and its endless amount of useful information.

Do You Require An Accountant?

Let's face it, we can't be good at everything and we can't be passionate about everything, and for me, accountancy is something I am neither good at nor passionate about. When we don't have that interest or natural skill with something, we tend to not put our all into it, and accountancy is something that is too important to be lazy with and risk getting wrong. This is why I personally think that having an accountant is a life saver. It allows you the opportunity to have someone on hand to guide you through your paperwork and to advise you on everything you need to know about running your business from the 'numbers' point of view, so that you don't have to figure it all out yourself.

What I do hope and assume, is that whether or not you are interested in the paperwork side of running a business, you are extremely keen to keep your business in profit. At the end of my first financial year, I found out that I had unfortunately made a loss. This is relatively common with new businesses in the first year, as arguably lots of money needs to go into the business to get the ball rolling, be it advertising or materials. You need to create a base for yourself and establish your business and you will not be making millions straight off the bat, and so if you do make a loss in your first year, try not to be disheartened. The general rule of thumb is that businesses make a loss in their first year, breakeven in the second year and make a profit in the third year.

This is also why having an accountant could be beneficial for yourself, as they could guide you and advise you on your income vs. outgoings to help you reach those yearly financial goals.

When running a business, paperwork is inevitable. Accounts, finances and VAT is inevitable. If you are like I was and are starting out with no idea about any of this, then do not panic...just follow my advice and watch your business succeed.

For starters, you need to establish how you are planning to keep track of your business finances. You need to choose an invoicing platform that is suitable for your business, such as Quickbooks, Sage or ZOHO Books. If you are really unsure about which platform is best, then this is the optimal time to check the gov.uk website for the list of HMRC-approved websites or introduce yourself to an account who can point you in the right direction for your specific business needs. These platforms are also useful for tracking your profit and loss, and for creating a paperless accountancy system, because you can also upload your expenses and business receipts onto it. Another benefit is that you have the ability to invite your accountant to oversee your accounts digitally, which means that your accountancy bill will be reduced as the accounts are all in one place online, reducing time spent searching through paperwork.

Alternatively, if you decide not to use accountancy software, I recommend having a physical spreadsheet in which you manually input your income and outgoings, this way you can see it all in front of you and you have total control of it. I believe that if you are physically writing something down, you are mentally more aware of what is being written. Whereas with automated platforms that input the information for you, it can arguably be easier to skip over the information. Knowing that you have to physically write down all of your expenses will also encourage you to remember to keep every receipt from every business transaction, as you will potentially need it as evidence of your expenses further down the line – this is so important. You can see an example of my own spreadsheet for KARD Graphic Design on the following page.

| Month | Self Employed | | | Employed |
	Professional fees	Expenses	Details e.g printing/ stationery/office equipment	

Having an accountant is beneficial in many ways more than just managing your finances. As soon as you have your financial structure in place and have found a system that works specifically for yourself, then your accountant is on hand to help this system run smoothly and consistently. Accountants are trained to know the ins and outs of managing your finances and they will always have the most up to date knowledge on everything under this category in business, so you don't need to.

Whether or not you decide to get yourself an accountant to help you along the way, the main points I want you to remember and act on from this section are:

- **ALWAYS keep your receipts from any business-related transaction (this can be digital or physical);**

- **Keep a close eye on your outgoings compared to your income, you want to make sure you end your financial years in profit;**

- Stay up to date with VAT and finance knowledge by checking regularly on government and VAT-related websites;

- In addition to registering with an accountancy/ invoicing platform, create a physical spreadsheet to track all of your finances manually (see my example).

CONCLUSION

Thank you for putting your trust in me and taking the time out of your busy schedule to read this book. I hope that you have taken in every piece of advice I have given you and I hope you apply my advice wherever necessary during your exciting new career. I am very excited for what is to come on your journey, and I encourage you to make the most of every opportunity that comes your way, take chances, meet people and most importantly, enjoy it!

This book highlights many important aspects of the exciting world of self-employment, including the importance of involving other knowledgeable people in your career, as no one is able to be good at everything – as much as we all may want to be! I have written about some of the most important people in my life, from family and friends, to tutors and mentors, as these people have helped me make it possible to run my graphic design business successful and have helped give me the confidence and push to believe in my abilities as a designer and businesswoman, and this is what I am to do for you through this book. Learn as you go along, whether it's a logo, a video, a website or a set of brand guidelines, follow my steps and start your success.

Keep this book close to you, refer to it whenever you may need to and whenever you feel doubt in your health, wellbeing and abilities, refer specifically to section 2 and remind yourself why you started this journey in the first place.

I wish you all the success in the world and I KNOW your business will thrive! Good luck!

EPILOGUE

I wrote this book during a very exciting and important time in my life, a time of extreme change that involved a lot of important decisions and a rollercoaster of emotions. Moving to Germany alone at the age of 22 was one of the biggest and scariest things I have ever done, but I will stand by it being one of the best life decisions I have made, and it has reminded me that the mindfulness advice given throughout this book is definitely not an ultimate cure for any negative feelings, as I am definitely not the finished article, and may never be. I have however, provided a very effective way of managing your emotions in the safest and healthiest way possible. A way that is proven to work.

Developing ourselves is a process, not an event. There is never an endpoint, and this is what you need to keep in mind. We will always go through whirlwind emotions and unpredictable situations and changes, and speaking for myself, we may never be one hundred percent satisfied with who we are. This means that there will always be new goals, new challenges and new hindrances. You need to be aware of this and be prepared to face these potentially unpredictable situations. The point of this book is to have a source in which you can refer back to time and time again to help yourself come out the other end stronger, happier, healthier and more successful.

I personally have revisited sections of this book (even during the process of writing it) to help keep myself on the right path and to remind myself of what I need to do to maintain my motivation and be more successful. As said before, this is a process and this is your own path that you are creating, and so it is important that you always remain the best version of yourself.

I grew up in a very small and quiet, yet extremely beautiful and inspirational part of the world. This came with both benefits and negatives. The positives are, as I mentioned, the beauty of my surroundings. Exmoor is, in my opinion, one of the most stunning and photogenic places I have ever seen, and I am extremely lucky to have it on my doorstep. This comes with (what seems to be) endless miles of countryside, hills and paths – both coastal and woodland. The point I am getting to here is, this 'endless' supply of beautiful walks and scenery was and always will be my happy place, the place where I go to think, to exercise, to be inspired, or even to just go to escape the phone signal and escape reality.

On the other hand, living in such a small community means that the amount of work available is extremely low, and so fight for what work is available is extremely high, which is why I made the decision to leave Somerset and go further afield to discover my true capabilities. This is what led me to Birmingham, and then Stuttgart.

Of course, there are times where I get homesick, fed up, lonely etc. but this is why I need to remind myself that these feelings are temporary, and this is why I need to find that 'happy place' wherever it is that I am living. In Birmingham, I definitely didn't have the luxury of Exmoor on my doorstep, however I had a 24-hour gym within walking distance from my house. Stuttgart appears to be a happy middle ground, with it being a city there are plenty of gyms available, as well as lots of beautiful country-side walks surrounding the city. Walking is a big love of mine, and so factoring this into where I want my business to be based is extremely important for my happiness and sanity.

Success is a choice, not luck.

You are the one that can determine your future and you are completely in control of it, even when it may not seem like it. I am well aware that I am not the finished article, I have a lot of room to grow and learn and I always will do, and so will you. Use your goals, aims, success, happiness, unhappiness etc... as a challenge, and never stop creating new challenges for yourself. My main goal when I began writing this book was to give people a shortcut to success, and now at the end of the book, my goal is still this to an extent. However, having our own wins and losses is all part of the process, and so my real goal with this book and from now on, is to help people, to advise people and to push people to learn and try new things every day, because that is also my personal goal.

What is Art?

I believe that everyone has a different interpretation of what Art is and what it means, but to me, art is a language and way of expressing feelings and emotions that are built up on the inside. Art is also a way of communicating without having to say a word.

For me, I believe that art is a talent that everyone carries but not everyone chooses to show or present an interest for. I believe that if everyone puts their mind to it, they will realise that art is a talent that they naturally have.

My interpretation of art is that it can help people see the world from many perspectives due to their own interpretations of what they see as a drawing. One drawing or painting can produce many views on everything and anything and it is up to the person viewing it to gain their own interpretation.

Art 'creates problems to solve' and answers its own questions. The process of sitting down and creating art comes from what is in people's minds and nothing else, which is why mistakes are made, as what is in people's minds may not be what they want to express in the physical art.

Graphic Design is a form of Art.

Kathryn Roberts

Useful Websites:

You will have noticed that throughout the book I referred to a large range of different websites. I would like to clarify that each website I have referred to has been used by either myself or a knowledgeable source. I have put all these websites in chapter order in an easy-to-find place below to save you having to search back through the book to find them.

Please note that some of the websites mentioned (e.g. outsourcing and timekeeping websites) are from my own personal preference and I would always recommend comparing them to others to find which ones work for you.

Section One – Providing a quality service

- www.getharvest.com
- www.gov.uk/government/organisations/intellectual-property-office

Section Two – Your health and wellbeing

- www.google.com/drive

Section Three – Outsourcing

- www.upwork.com
- www.fiverr.com
- www.freelancer.com

Section Four – Social Media

- www.wix.com
- www.wordpress.com
- www.squarespace.com

Section Five – Marketing & Business

- www.gov.uk
- www.quickbooks.intuit.com
- www.sage.com
- www.zoho.com
- https://www.gov.uk/working-for-yourself

If you have any feedback, comments, questions, require any advice, or are interested in collaboration, please do not hesitate to get in contact with the details below:

Kathryn Annice Roberts

KARD Graphic Design

Web: www.kardesign.org

Mail: kathrynrobertsdesign@outlook.com

CLIENT FEEDBACK

"Thanks so much for introducing us to Kathryn. She has done a brilliant job for us and worked incredibly hard on it all. She is a great ambassador for your course and the School of Vis Com."
Dr Sarah Jones, Head of Birmingham School of Media.

"Well done Kathryn, you did us proud!"

Nathan Tromans MA SFHEA, Associate Professor, Head of School, School of Visual Communication.
Following the annual review book created by KARD Graphic Design for the Birmingham School of Media.

"Brilliant customer service as usual"
Greg Newlands, Greg Newlands Fitness

"I actually love them and can't wait to get them up and selling"
Matthew Storer, Founder of The Woody & Winter Foundation
Following the design of roller banners for the charity, amongst other marketing materials.

Very happy with the logo and marketing materials received from Kathryn, would highly recommend."
Adelle Morgan, High Calibre Cleaning

"Great logo designed with lots of options to choose from. Highly recommend. 5*"
Michael Webber Griffiths, Teddie Boy Charters

"Katie kindly helped us create a fabulous calendar to raise money for Macmillan. The end result is a good high-quality calendar"
Andrea Rathbone, Macmillan Cancer Support

ACKNOWLEDGMENTS

There are so many people who have supported me and helped me on my journey, I am extremely lucky to say that there are too many to write. I've met so many amazing people and made some friends for life and I am very grateful for each and every person who has contributed to my success and supported me. I would like to acknowledge and thank a small number of these people; this book is written as a massive thank you to them.

Keith Crocker – Keith was my art teacher during my years at West Somerset College. He could see my passion for art and design and massively pushed me to reach my potential. Although I didn't continue art and design at university and further, my style of art massively evolved in college with inspiration from graphic and geometrical artists such as Wassily Kandinsky. Keith noticed this and helped to push me to continue this style of working, and this led me to make my decision to turn these geometric paintings and drawings into digital work on a computer screen, also known as graphic design. Thanks a lot Keith.

A Kandinsky-inspired acrylic painting on thick, 50x60cm wood.
Year 13, West Somerset College

David Osbaldestin – David was my personal university tutor for both my first and final year at Birmingham City University (BCU). My first meeting with David was actually during my applicant day, where myself and my mum saw BCU for the very first time. As usual, we were lost and couldn't find where we were meant to be and David was the one who rescued us and told us where we needed to be – it just so happened that he was teaching on the course I wanted to join and by chance ended up being my tutor and personal inspiration during my years at BCU. David pushed me to try out many different artistic techniques from filmmaking, to photography, to editorial design and to entering competitions and successfully approaching clients. I want to say a big thank you to David for his determination to push me to my full potential and having the confidence in me, especially during my final year when I had lost all my coursework weeks before my deadlines. I also want to thank him for his continuous honesty, an example being again, in my final year during the dissertation writing process, I'll never forget the confrontation during our first dissertation meeting where the first words he said were 'were you angry when you wrote this? Has the university done something to wind you up?' But thanks to David, I am now living the dream as a graphic designer with a degree I am extremely proud of.

My University Dissertation as a published book. My first leap into the world of book publishing and a huge inspiration for this book.

My Older Sister, Ali – Ali and I have ultimately chosen to go down completely different career paths. She is now leading a successful career as a primary school teacher, which was her childhood dream. Not only am I super proud of Ali for achieving her dreams, but I am also very grateful for her. She has helped me to explore a brand-new niche for me. This being the design of unique teaching resources. Ali and I have been working together on a few of her resources which has led to a lot of positive feedback both for her and myself. When Ali was a teenager, she spent time living and working in Germany, which led her to fall in love with the German culture and become a fluent German speaker. Her achievements here are what inspired me to also take up the German language in college and what gave me the confidence to also find work in Germany, and it is one of the best things I have ever done so far in my life. So, for this I would like to thank Ali hugely.

An example of a fun image created for Ali's reception children.

My Parents, Dave and Liz – My final acknowledgment goes to my parents. My mum did a similar thing to me a few years ago, she took the plunge and became freelance and has since, made a huge success of it, and I have never seen her happier. One major difference though, is that she did this following 40 years working a secure job in a widely known pharmaceuticals company. Her passion for work and determination to succeed has always been an inspiration to me. It's so reassuring to have such a strong character to call my mum and I want to thank her for everything she's done throughout my life. My Dad moved down to Somerset at 16 years of age to begin his long-lasting and highly successful career as a charter boat skipper and to this day is still making a success of it. This is something I cannot ignore and something that gives me huge confidence that working for yourself is such a rewarding thing to do. Much like my mum, dad is also a strong and passionate individual who always gets the job finished to an exceptional standard – something that I also aspire to every day. Without the help and push from my parents from a very young age, I would definitely not be where I am today and for this, I would like to thank them from the bottom of my heart.

The Roberts Family, 2020.

Printed in Great Britain
by Amazon

85782755R10061